Amazing You

Dreams

Theresa Cheung

h

a division of Hodder Headline Limited

Sharp writing for smart people

Welcome to *AMAZING YOU - DREAMS*

We hope that understanding your dreams helps your wishes to come true.

Also available are *Astrology*, *Numerology*, *Psychic Powers* and *Spells* – there are lots more to come in the *Amazing You* series and you can be the first to discover them!

BITE HERE!

Wanna join the gang? All the latest news, gossip and prize giveaways from BITE! PLUS more information on new titles in the *Amazing You* series.

Sign up NOW to join the BITE gang, and get a limited edition denim BITE bag or an exclusive preview copy of a brand new teen title, long before it's available in the shops.

To sign up text DREAMS to 60022

or go to **www.bookswithbite.co.uk**

FREE! Win your very own dreamcatcher.
For your chance, text DREAMER to 60022 now!

Texting costs your normal rate, texts from Bite are free.
You can unsubscribe at any time by texting BITE STOP.
Terms & Conditions Apply. For details go to www.bookswithbite.co.uk

About the series

Amazing You is our stunning new Mind Body Spirit series. It shows you how to make the most of your life and boost your chances of success and happiness. You'll discover some fantastic things about you and your friends by trying out the great tips and fun exercises. See for yourself just how amazing you can be!

Available now
Astrology
Dreams
Numerology
Psychic Powers
Spells

Coming soon
Crystals
Face and Hand Reading
Fortune Telling
Graphology

Acknowledgements

My thanks to the hundreds of children and young adults I've talked to over the years. Your curiosity, freshness and insight were my inspiration while writing this book. A big thank you to my editor, Anne Clark, for her encouragement and positive energy. Many thanks to everyone at Hodder Children's Books for making this project happen, in particular Katie Sergeant for her help and support. And finally, many thanks to my partner Ray and my children, Robert and Ruth, for their love, enthusiasm and patience while I went into exile to complete this project.

About the author

Theresa Cheung was born into a family of psychics, astrologers and numerologists. She gave her first public numerology reading at the age of fourteen, and has been involved in the serious study of the psychic arts for over twenty years. As a former English secondary school teacher and health and fitness instructor Theresa has worked with many young adults. She contributes regularly to women's magazines, such as *Red*, *She* and *Here's Health*, and is the author of over twenty health, popular psychology, humour and New Age books including *Dreams*, *Numerology* and *Face and Hand Reading* in the *Amazing You* series.

Text copyright © Theresa Cheung 2004
Illustrations copyright © Jo Quinn/Inkshed.co.uk 2004
Cover illustration © Monica Laita 2004

Editor: Katie Sergeant
Book design by Don Martin
Cover design: Hodder Children's Books

Published in Great Britain in 2004
by Hodder Children's Books

The right of Theresa Cheung to be identified as the author of this Work
and Jo Quinn as the illustrator of this Work has been asserted by them
in accordance with the Copyright, Designs and Patents Act 1988.

All rights reserved. Apart from any use permitted under UK copyright
law, this publication may only be reproduced, stored or transmitted, in
any form, or by any means with prior permission in writing of the
publishers or in the case of reprographic production in accordance with
the terms of licences issued by the Copyright Licensing Agency.

A catalogue record for this book is available from the British Library.

10 9 8 7 6 5 4 3 2 1

ISBN: 0340882360

Printed and bound by Bookmarque Ltd, Croydon, Surrey

The paper and board used in this paperback by Hodder Children's Books
are natural recyclable products made from wood grown in sustainable
forests. The manufacturing processes conform to the environmental
regulations of the country of origin.

Hodder Children's Books
a division of Hodder Headline Limited
338 Euston Road, London NW1 3BH

Contents

Introduction: In your dreams

The only person really qualified to interpret your dreams is you. With this book's help you can learn to read the symbolism and hidden messages of your dreams with skill and accuracy. You'll begin an exciting relationship with your dream world that is just as alive and valid as the one you have with your waking world. And, best of all, you'll discover how to turn your dreams into creative and helpful experiences that can help you solve problems and improve your chances of success in life and happiness.

A wonderful journey of self-discovery awaits you as you explore the mysterious and fascinating world of your dreams. Enjoy every sleeping and waking moment of it!

CHAPTER ONE

Life is but a dream

We are such stuff
As dreams are made on, and our little life
Is rounded with a sleep.

William Shakespeare, *The Tempest*

We all dream. If you are one of those people who say they don't, you do, the fact is you just can't remember. In an average lifetime, a person will spend approximately twenty-five years asleep and experience at least 300,000 dreams. It's been estimated by sleep lab studies that babies dream the most but young people, like you, come a close second, dreaming for four or five hours a night, while an adult may only get an hour or so.

The dreaming mind

When you sleep your body repairs itself, and your brain 'processes' the events of your day, mixing them up with previous experiences. Every night we experience four or five different sleep stages that are designed to prepare us for a new day. These are distinguished by the frequency of brain waves, eye movement and muscle tension. The sleep stage in which dreaming occurs is called rapid eye movement sleep or (REM).

Scientists tell us that dreaming is essential to our mental, emotional and physical health and well-being because dreams can help us relax, release frustrations, sort out information, solve problems or alert us to them, play out fantasies, offer inspiration and restore balance. Dreams can do all this but they can offer even more besides. Once you know how to understand and work with them they can be an invisible and powerful inner resource that can enrich your life considerably. No-one knows how but dreams seem to be able to link your conscious (waking) mind with the hidden part of your mind,

2

often called the 'unconscious', 'sixth sense' or 'intuition'. You may like to think of your unconscious as your inner guide that just seems to know what is the best thing for you to do.

⋆⅄ DROPPING OFF ...

Because sleeping and dreaming are so crucial, your brain may sometimes demand the sleep it needs for regeneration and processing of information so that you don't go into mental or physical overload. That's why you may suddenly drop off for no apparent reason when you're watching TV at home or when travelling by car or train.

If you do find that you sometimes need a quick nap during the day, don't worry about it. Tell yourself that you are processing your thoughts and recharging your batteries. Naps are excellent times for dreams – as long as you nap somewhere safe and warm, and not in the middle of a lesson! Any time of day that you can sneak in a nap is potential extra dreamtime. Not only that but dreams from different times of the day have different qualities. You can have lots of fun investigating this possibility.

People have always been fascinated by dreams and what they mean. Here's a brief history of dream analysis to give you some background to this ancient practice.

A history of dream interpretation

The earliest known dream dictionary dates back about 4,000 years. Now called the Chester Beatty Papyrus, it came from Thebes in Upper Egypt and is kept in the British Museum. In the Chester Beatty Papyrus dreams are interpreted and translated as prophecies or omens. For example, if you dream that your teeth fall out, your loved ones are trying to kill you!

In ancient Greece dreams were also thought to be lucky or unlucky predictions. In about AD 200 Artimidorus, a dream interpreter living in Asia Minor, Greece, wrote a book about dream interpretation which is still in print today.

The approach to dreams as good or bad omens continued for several hundred years until the fifteenth century when dreams were no longer regarded as significant or important. Even Shakespeare called them 'children of the idle brain.' This school of thought persisted into the nineteenth century, when dreams were still thought to be meaningless. Then along came Freud and Jung, two men who have had the greatest impact on the way we look at dreams today.

Sigmund Freud (1856-1939) opened the door to the scientific study of dreams with his book *The Interpretation of Dreams*. His ideas have now become outdated but when he called dreams the 'royal road to the unconscious' he paved the way for the work of Carl Jung (1875-1961). Jung found common dream themes that ran through every culture. These themes or archetypes existed within what he called the 'collective unconscious', a source of shared knowledge that exists within us all. His theories on the collective unconscious redefined psychology and made it accessible to ordinary people, like you and me.

Dream interpretation is as popular today as it has ever been, with people from all walks of life using dreams as unique and very personal sources of guidance and inspiration. There are many approaches to the study and analysis of dreams and they are increasingly regarded as tools for change, growth and well-being. But ultimately you will discover that working with and interpreting dreams is as individual as you are.

Just a little word of caution: don't get too carried away with analyzing your dreams. They are a fascinating part of what makes up amazing you, but you should always keep your feet on the ground and use your common sense and good judgement as well. Use what you learn about your dreams wisely and you'll soon see the benefits. Read on to find out about different types of dreams and what they can do for you ...

CHAPTER TWO

Types of dreams

Just as there are different kinds of singers – rock, ballad, pop, rap and soul – there are different kinds of dreams. Some are the 'sorting out and organizing' ones, some are reminders, some try to answer questions or solve problems and some give us clues to the future. They can be broken down into different categories as follows.

✳ DAILY PROCESSING DREAMS

Also known as factual dreams, daily processing dreams usually occur as soon as you fall asleep. These are dreams in which you go over and over things that happened during the day, especially

things that were repetitive or forced you to concentrate. Dreaming about exams or a tough homework assignment is a typical example of this kind of dream. Usually you don't remember much of these dreams, but when you do you can easily connect them with activities in your life.
Processing dreams are not usually laden with meaning. They often tend to be memories in picture form of something that happened in your day – a conversation you had or a scene you saw. Think of them as bits and pieces of information that your brain is sorting and filing by night.

✕✕ VIGILANT DREAMS

These are processing dreams that involve your senses. For example, if your mobile rings or a picture falls to the ground with a banging sound while you are asleep, that sound is incorporated into your dream but often appears as something else, such as a police siren rushing to an emergency. The smell of flowers in your room might become a garden scene in your dream.

This kind of dream shows that even though you are asleep, your brain continues to receive and process information through your senses.

✳⅄ PROBLEM-SOLVING DREAMS

Your unconscious – that part of your mind that lies below your conscious awareness – knows all your problems and it usually knows how to solve them. If the unconscious thinks a solution is important enough you'll get a problem-solving dream. You can usually recognize these dreams by the feelings they bring. You may, like Colette in the following dream, feel an 'ahh' of recognition or chills or goose bumps when you link the message it contains to your problem.

Colette had recently started at a new school. She was missing her old friends and way of life and didn't feel that she would ever fit in. Eventually she started to make a few friends but the real

9

breakthrough came when she had a dream that spoke clearly to her. In her dream, Colette saw a girl sobbing her heart out because she had spilled a drink. Colette told the girl that it wasn't the end of the world – she could just buy another drink. The girl said that she didn't want another drink – she only wanted the one she had spilled.

When Colette woke up she realized she was acting like the girl in her dream, and it was time to for her to stop looking backwards, enjoy her new friendships and move forward with her life.

Have you said, or heard someone say, 'sleep on it' before making up your mind? It's a wise statement. Even if you don't get an obvious answer to a problem, you might well find that after one of these problem-solving dreams you feel different. In the morning you can take a fresh view of the situation and be a little more objective. You may not even know what has happened, but you will feel more confident and in control. So the next time you feel anxious, uncertain or upset, try 'sleeping on it' before you take action.

✳⅄ CREATIVE OR WISH FULFILMENT DREAMS

This kind of dream is very similar to a problem-solving dream in that it creates a space where your mind can be more objective and inspirational. A creative dream can give you the answer or the idea you have been looking for. They can be very exciting and motivating dreams giving you the confidence and self-belief to do what you really believe in. These dreams may even unlock hidden talents that you didn't know you had, proving that your unconscious can be creative if you just relax and let it guide you.

Many famous artists, writers, musicians, mathematicians and scientists have used creative dreaming as their inspiration. One night, in 1816, Mary Shelley, her husband the poet Shelley and a group of friends were telling ghost stories, when Lord Byron challenged them to write a horror story. That night Mary Shelley dreamed of the creature that would become Frankenstein's monster in the book she later wrote. Other famous literary dreamers include Edgar Allan Poe, Samuel Taylor Coleridge, Charlotte Brontë, Robert Louis Stevenson, J. R. R. Tolkien and J. K. Rowling. Paul McCartney heard a haunting melody in one of his dreams, confirmed that none of the Beatles had heard it before and wrote it down. It became the tune for the famous song 'Yesterday'. Inventions and ideas that have sprung from dreams include: the model of the atom, the M9 analogue computer, the isolation of insulin in the treatment of diabetes, and the sewing machine.

However, you don't have to dream creatively to build a better toaster or write a masterpiece. If you have an everyday problem creative dreaming can help you. See Paula's dilemma below:

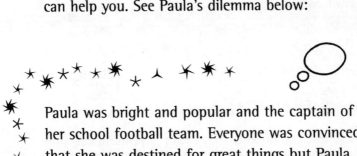

Paula was bright and popular and the captain of her school football team. Everyone was convinced that she was destined for great things but Paula didn't have a clue what she wanted to do with her life. She didn't want to go to university. Her parents became worried and suggested that she see the school's careers advisor. It took only one session and Paula started to feel drawn towards work in the leisure industry where she could use both her mental and sporting skills. But the real breakthrough came when she had a dream that convinced her she was on the right path. In the dream she was in a huge hall with hundreds of people. They all seemed bored and unhappy and Paula somehow got them to work in teams and participate in games. The atmosphere in the room changed from boredom to excitement. The dream

was confirming that Paula was thinking
along the right lines. Now she felt confident,
motivated and focused on her choice
of career.

✴⅄ PSYCHOLOGICAL DREAMS

These are dreams that bring psychological 'junk'
to our attention – the things that we would
rather not think about. Instead of helping us solve
a problem or make a decision, psychological
dreams make us face something about ourselves
that might be blocking us from moving forward.
They are often about our fears, anxieties,
resentments, guilt and insecurities. See what
Chloe's dream brought to her attention ...

One night, Chloe dreamt that she was in a cage
with lots of mice. She found herself running
around and around on the wheel in the cage, and
the mice were pushing it faster and faster so that

she had to run for her life, for if she fell off she was sure she was going to be eaten. In her everyday life, Chloe often felt as if she was running from one thing to another, with no time to take a break. She had this disturbing dream on the night she had come home from a full day at school, followed by athletics practice, choir practice and then babysitting for her aunt while helping her boyfriend revise for his exams. During the day her head teacher had given her a telling-off for falling behind with her schoolwork. So not only did she get a reprimand from her head teacher, but her inner guide was telling her off too. She realized that she needed to relax more and to learn to not take on so much.

Some psychological dreams are nightmares and others are extremely vivid. Sometimes they are repetitive as if your dreaming mind is telling you to wake up and listen. Like problem-solving dreams you need to pay attention to them and look for their message.

✶人 NIGHTMARES

Nightmares can occur at any age but research has shown that you are more likely to experience them as a child or in your teens. You may have had the common dream where you are falling from a great height, or monsters are chasing you, or someone is attacking you and you are terrified and can't find anywhere to hide. You wake up and you are still shaking with fear, perhaps sweating and your heart is pounding. Even though you know it is just a dream it can take some time before you can relax again and go back to sleep.

Nightmares are the result of inner fears which have been triggered by something – perhaps an argument with your mum and dad or a friend, exam stress, a ghost film before bed, or simply feeling scared of someone or something. But nightmares aren't always caused by anxiety –

they can also be caused by physical stress, such as a heavy meal before bed or a temperature when you are feeling under the weather. Similarly a pain that is not sufficient to wake you but is nevertheless disturbing may be symbolized in your dream as a thorn in the flesh, a wild animal biting where the pain is and so on. Stomach and digestive complaints often produce dreams about disputes, while the pounding of a hammer in a dream can signal a headache.

✶⅄ PRECOGNITIVE DREAMS

This type of dream is one in which you see the future before it happens. For example, you dream about someone you really like but haven't the courage to approach, and the next day you run into them and they ask you out! Many precognitive dreams, however, are symbolic, which means they speak to you in a kind of code language that you need to interpret. For instance, you dream about being handed a bouquet of flowers and a few days later your friends throw a surprise party in your honour. Flowers often represent congratulations or recognition in some way.

Even though many dream dictionaries do describe all dream images as omens or images of the future, most dream researchers agree that precognitive dreams are rare. When they do occur, they often have a strange quality. Maybe the light is strange, the objects unusual, or oddly shaped, or the landscape is peculiar. Having said that, there have been many instances when people claim to have dreamt of things before they happen. Many people, for example, dreamt about the 9/11 disaster before it happened. You may also have heard or read about people who cancelled train trips or flights because of a foreboding dream, or people who dreamt of the winning numbers before winning the lottery. Often precognitive dreams may be about more commonplace things, such as Sarah's dream ...

Sarah and her best friend, Jessica, spent a lot of time together, both in and out of school, so it wasn't surprising that she had a dream about the two of them travelling on a train together. But Jessica's ticket was different from Sarah's. Sarah was going to school but Jessica was going to America.

A month later Jessica told Sarah about her plans to travel to America in her gap year. Sarah had a spooky feeling that she'd heard that somewhere before!

⋆⅄ RECURRING DREAMS

Recurring dreams involve the same action, scenery, people and things. You may be taking part or you may be watching the action. This type of dream may only happen a few times or it may become a regular occurrence. One explanation has come

from people who research past lives. They suggest
that recurring dreams are memories from past lives
that have lingered for some reason – and the
dreamer needs to work out why. Far more likely
though, is that this kind of dream tries to attract
your attention to something that needs sorting
out in your life. It is important to remember the
details of such dreams so that if any variations
occur they can give you clues as to how things
are working out in your waking life.

Recurring dreams, or recurring elements in
your dreams, that are typical for young people
involve: monsters, wild animals, something
ordinary turning sinister and giving chase, flying,
breathing underwater, burying a dead body, the
death of a parent or a repetitive task that must
be performed at the command of monsters,
zombies or gangsters. In chapter eight you'll
find typical recurring dream elements like the
ones mentioned above discussed in more detail
to help you understand more about your
situation and feelings.

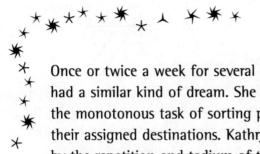

Once or twice a week for several months Kathryn had a similar kind of dream. She had to perform the monotonous task of sorting parts of bodies to their assigned destinations. Kathryn feels numbed by the repetition and tedium of the task. During her dream she is annoyed about the unfairly heavy workload but not the macabre nature of the task. It is only when she wakes up that she feels appalled by the grisly details it contained.

At the time she was having this recurring dream Kathryn was working extremely hard at school. Inevitably other aspects of her life, such as her family, friends and social life, suffered. When it was pointed out to her that this kind of dream often reflects the stress that is felt when someone strives constantly to achieve and to meet standards that are unforgiving and relentless, Kathryn started to think about how she needed to take some time out now and again to restore some balance in her life.

✴⋋ FLYING DREAMS

Seven out of ten people experience the sensation of flying in their dreams at least once in their life. It is the most exhilarating feeling and not at all frightening. Using your arms as wings, you may travel in your dreams from your bedroom into the street, soar above the treetops and the oceans, or be transported to other places, times and worlds. You may even bring back information that could not have been discovered in any other way about the places you have visited. One explanation is that during sleep your spirit leaves your body, but, whatever the cause a flying dream is liberating. It shows that the dreamer wishes or is able to rise above his or her problems or restrictions.
Dreaming of flying during a heavy bout of exams, for example, could suggest your resilience and ability to handle the pressure.

Have you ever fallen asleep and had the feeling that you were floating and looking down at your body sleeping? This experience is far more common than you think. It isn't strictly a dream, but an out-of-the-body experience, but the feeling of floating can be similar to dream-flying. Once again this should reassure you that there is so much more to your life than just the physical. Whether you have experienced this or not, don't be frightened. When and if it happens it feels quite normal and isn't at all scary because you will feel peaceful and calm.

TELEPATHY

Telepathic communication can take place during dreams. Some dream experts believe that when we dream of someone we have not thought about for some time, there is a good chance they will be thinking of us. Sometimes the message is one of pain, fear or distress. Sally's dream provides a good example of this. Sally woke up at 2 am from a dream in which she saw her best friend, Kelly, crying her heart out. The next morning she telephoned her friend's house and Kelly told her tearfully that her boyfriend had dumped her by a 2 am text message.

✴⅄ FALSE AWAKENINGS

Dreams are memories, so it is often difficult to be certain if an event really occurred in a dream. I've once been so convinced that I had booked a ticket for a musical that I telephoned the box office to ask where I would be sitting. I was told that there was no reservation in my name!

Other examples of false awakenings include things that go bump in the night, such as strange noises or seeing things at the end of your bed. Who and whatever it is that we see and hear is so real and the memory so clear that in the morning we believe it to be real and not a dream – but a dream it is.

⋆⅄ WALKING AND TALKING IN YOUR SLEEP

Sleepwalking, or moving in your sleep, is an attempt to put a dream into action. Most likely you have grown out of the habit, if you ever had it, but if an extremely stressful occasion arises, we may, like Lady Macbeth, reenact the nightmare in this way. Talking in your sleep is an attempt to verbally continue a dream. You are more likely to walk, talk or move in your sleep when you are under mental pressure. Most of the time this is totally harmless but some sleepwalkers and talkers can put themselves in real danger. Precautions should therefore be taken. Make sure windows are closed and doors locked, remove potential obstacles from the floor and try to have the bedroom on the ground floor if you can, to avoid the dangers of stairs. If you're really worried about your sleepwalking seek advice from your doctor. If you meet someone who is sleepwalking don't try to wake them up – just guide them quietly and gently back to bed.

So there you have it – the different types of
dreams. Do you recognize the common theme of
self-awareness? Whatever kind of dream you have
the purpose is usually the same – to help you
figure out who you are. You may not think much
about self-awareness, but it is absolutely essential.
If you don't know yourself, you could be easily
swayed by what other people think you should be,
do, say and think. That can interfere with your
ability to make decisions, find happiness and
accomplish what YOU want in life. Always listen
to what you know is the right choice for you and
you'll discover just how amazing you can be.

CHAPTER THREE

Interpreting your dreams

Have you ever wondered why dreams are so difficult to make sense of? It's because the information they contain is presented in a language of images – of people alive or dead, known and unknown; animals both domestic and wild; landscapes and buildings familiar and strange; or any number of symbolic images such as jewellery, food, clothing and so on. You may also dream of celebrities or other famous people, past or present. The number of images that your dream mind can produce is endless! It may seem complicated but try to think of dream images as a language that your mind uses to make sense of your life.

Symbols and images are your own thoughts, feelings and ideas turned into a series of pictures, like ordinary scenes in your daily life. For example, if you feel overwhelmed you may have a dream where you are swimming but finding it hard to keep your head above water. If you feel confused you may have a dream where you are wondering about lost in a dark forest. Most of these images can only really be interpreted by you. Some, however, are common to everyone, or can be universally recognized. We will take a closer look at some general symbols in chapter nine.

Pictures from your past

Your unconscious mind is working all the time using images, feelings and pictures from your past and linking them with something that may have happened recently in real life – perhaps to remind you of something. For example, if you dream of an episode that happened years ago something about it might remind you of current events. Just as it did for Jenny ...

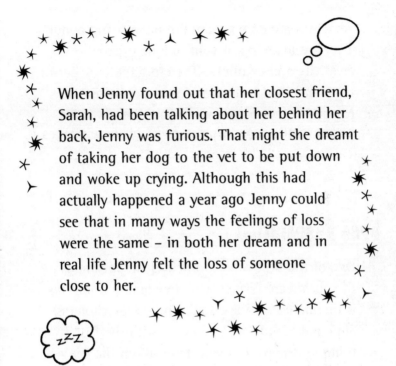

When Jenny found out that her closest friend, Sarah, had been talking about her behind her back, Jenny was furious. That night she dreamt of taking her dog to the vet to be put down and woke up crying. Although this had actually happened a year ago Jenny could see that in many ways the feelings of loss were the same – in both her dream and in real life Jenny felt the loss of someone close to her.

To make sense of all the bits and pieces of your dreams you need to shift your perception and approach. But it always helps to recall the feelings you experienced in the dream for these give you the biggest clue to the interpretation. Dreams are completely personal. Your mind creates them and they are what they are because of who you are,

29

what you are doing, wanting, or worrying about. They are made up of your unique experiences, creativity and emotions. Therefore the only person really qualified to interpret your dreams is YOU. No-one knows better where your dreams come from or what they mean than you.

Free association

One of the best ways to uncover the meanings of your dream images is by free association. This is the method made popular by the psychologist Sigmund Freud. You simply go with the first thing that pops into your mind when the trigger word is given.

To get you going let's try some free association exercises.

Here are the numbers 1 to 10. Grab a notebook and pen and jot down the first word that comes to you when you think about them:

1...

2...

3...

4...

5...

6...

7...

8...

9...

10...

Here are some common colours. Jot down what they mean to you:

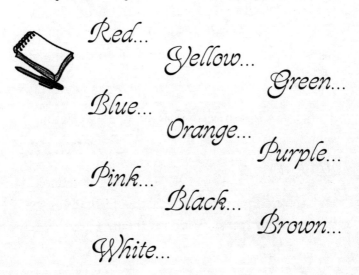

Red...

Yellow...

Green...

Blue...

Orange...

Purple...

Pink...

Black...

Brown...

White...

Now let's try the free association method with common terms you encounter every day. Write down what comes immediately to mind as a meaning for that word. Don't think too much, just write! If nothing pops into your head move on to the next word. Don't be tempted use dream dictionaries or turn to chapter nine to look up words – the idea is to start to get into the habit of thinking about your own personal associations for these words that may act as symbols in your dreams:

Aeroplane...

Balloon...

Book...

Chair...

Church...

Computer...

Door...

Flower...

Food...

Hat...

House...

Kiss...

Knife...

Letter...

Mirror...

Money...

Past...

River...

Sky...

Sugar...

Sun...

Telephone...

Television...

Train...

Tree...

Water...

Zoo...

Now try the free association exercise with animals, both wild and domestic. Make a list of as many as you can think of – you can include insects and birds too. If you prefer you can use free association with anything or anyone: your parents, siblings, friends, teachers, celebrities, landscapes, buildings, clothes, jewellery and food. Try to connect with your own personal associations: these may be symbols in your dreams.

DREAM ASSOCIATIONS

The next time you dream, use the free association method to help you get at the meaning of your dream images. If you don't immediately get an associative thought work through all your experiences with the images. For example, say you saw a caterpillar in a dream. Do you like caterpillars or do you find them a bit creepy? Try to discover what the image means to you right now, for the meanings of your symbols will change over time.

The more you work with your dreams the more familiar you will become with your personal images. You'll probably find that you dream the most about the things that you are familiar with and see every day: your friends, your family, your teachers, and your pets. Each time you dream about these familiar things they will have personal significance to you alone.

The great majority of dreams are not to be taken literally. You need to do a bit of detective work to get to the real message. Just because you dream that a friend is dying does not mean that he or she is about to die. In fact, interpreting dreams literally can be harmful. That's why it isn't a good idea to rely on a dream dictionary. What a dog means to you and what a dog means to someone else might be very different. Always bear in mind that your dream symbols and images are unique to you.

The images and symbols in your dreams aren't meant to be mystifying. They are simply trying to get their message across in the best way that they can. If you do find yourself getting tense or frustrated when analyzing your dreams this will block your connections. Take a break and try

again the next day. The subject of dream
interpretation needs to be approached with an
open mind and in a relaxed state.

You don't need to interpret every single dream
you have. Just like some films which are more
thought provoking than others, some dreams, like
those when you fly into outer space, or attend
a concert, are simply to be enjoyed. You don't
always have to dig deep for meaning. It's good
to be aware that a dream might contain a
message of importance and interpret what you
can but don't become obsessed with finding
meanings for every single detail. And when you
do think you have found the message, don't be
too quick to jump to conclusions. You don't have
to follow your dreams slavishly; remember that
your actions in your waking life are just as, if
not more, important.

CHAPTER FOUR

Remembering your dreams

Many of us forget our dreams immediately on waking. There is just so much to do when a new day starts and we neglect the wonderful world of meaning our dreams can reveal to us. This is a terrible shame. According to a Jewish Proverb: 'An unremembered dream is like an unopened letter from God.'

Remembering and understanding what you are saying to yourself in a dream is very important; once you realize that dreams are inner sources of help, offering guidance and inspiration, there is no reason why you can't use them to boost your chances of happiness and success in life. When you take an active interest in your dreams and learn how to interpret them, it's like having an inner guide or wise friend that is always there to offer you advice, support and guidance. And the more attention you pay to your dreams, by thinking about them, writing them down, and working with them, the more you will gain from your dream life. You will dream more, remember more and your dreams will speak more clearly to you.

To work with your dreams, which really means another aspect of your self, you do need to remember them. The fact that you make an effort to do this seems to remind your unconscious in some way, and even those who say they don't ever dream sometimes find that images from their dreams pop into their head during the day. Keeping a dream journal and recording your dreams as soon as you wake up will help your dream recall. The best book you will ever read on dreams and dreaming is the one you write yourself. So why not start a dream journal today?

Your dream journal

There is no one way to keep a dream diary but it might help if you follow a few simple, practical guidelines.

Make a commitment

Make an effort to buy a special notebook and pen that you just use for writing down your dreams. This simple task will alert your unconscious to the fact that you want to hear what it has to say. Once you have your pen and journal put them beside your bed and keep them in the same place at all times.

Speed

Some dreams fade quickly from memory so it is crucial you capture them as soon as you can. Immediately on waking write down your dream or dreams – even if this is in the middle of the night.

Don't brush your teeth first, call a friend or leave it till your alarm clock goes off. If you do that you'll probably forget all about it and will lose a valuable dream. Get into the habit of recording your dreams as soon as you wake up. Write down all that you can, if the dream is very long you can fill in the details later.

Number, time and date

Number each dream that you have so you can see how many dreams you experience each night and how many over a period of time. You will find that this varies constantly according to the time of the year, month and personal problems.

Write down the time on waking. This encourages serial dreaming. For example, if you wake at 4 am and write down a dream, you may find that you continue it at a later time or date.

The date of each dream is important too. On looking back you may find that some turn out to be prophetic but at the time of dreaming you didn't realize that they were.

Atmosphere, mood and setting

The atmosphere or mood of a dream is the most important aspect of your dream – in other words the feel of the dream. It can colour your day and give you a clue to its meaning. Even if you can't remember much of your dream write down your mood or how you are feeling. This will give you a clue as to the theme and message of your dream. If it was happy your day starts on a good note; if it was gloomy you may feel as if you have got out of bed on the wrong side; if you felt apprehensive then the day ahead may feel like a stressful one.

Theme

Look for the theme of your dream next. This reveals the subject under observation: the reason for your dream. It may be a holiday, a journey, an exam, or it may be waiting for someone or something, or even hope for the future such as meeting the guy of your dreams. Discovering the subject helps give your dream a title. For example, school dreams, celebrity dreams, holiday dreams and so on.

Characters, objects, signs and symbols

Make a note of the people in your dream. Some
will be known to you, some won't. Unknowns
often represent someone else or symbolize certain
things in our lives. A nurse, for example, could
stand for loving care, just as your sister in your
dream may not actually be drawing attention to
your sister but to sisterly qualities in you.

Dream characters could also be familiar
animals, such as cats and dogs, but others could
be unknown or shapeless entities that chase or
befriend you. When thinking about what they
mean use the free association technique (see
pages 30–34 to remind yourself). What do pigs,
cows, gods, ghosts and cats mean to you? The
shapeless monsters could well be aspects of
yourself that you are running away from.

When looking for objects note any cars, trees,
carrots, cups etc. Each will have a special meaning
in your dream language. You may well find
unrecognizable objects. Could these represent your
desire for change, for new experiences or for a
more exciting life?

Signs and symbols will often appear in your dreams. Signs act as signposts, suggesting possible directions for you to follow in life, whereas symbols offer glimpses of your inner world where the answers to many of your problems lie.

Movement and travel

Most dreams are action packed and frequently involve travelling, which suggests your way through life. The way you travel in a dream can reveal a lot about the amount of effort you are putting into your life, whether you are in the backseat or in control of your own driving force. Walking and running suggest that your self-generated effort stands you in good stead, whereas travelling on a crowded bus, train or plane could suggest that you are getting carried along with everyone else and it is time to stand on your own two feet. Bus stops, stations and airports are places of rest but you don't really want to hang around there for too long and need to make up your mind about where you are going.

Colours, sounds and conversations

Colours are often linked to atmosphere and mood in dreams. An overall grey scene suggests a dull mood or situation. Reds and oranges, on the other hand, offer hope and inspiration. In chapter nine you'll think more about the special significance of colours in your dreams and what you can learn about yourself from them.

Conversations and sounds in dreams can at first appear to be nonsense, but many words may be in code or have double meanings. Since you are the dreamer the clue to understanding them lies within you. Do certain phrases or snippets of conversations recur in your dreams? You can look back over your dream journal to see if any patterns start to emerge and draw your own conclusions from there. These messages might be of particular significance and your dreaming mind could be making sure you're paying attention to them.

Previous associations

Events from the day before or further back in
your past often appear in dreams a bit like action
replay. You may often find that scenes from
your favourite TV show are used by your
dreaming mind to convey something to you
or alert you to a particular problem, hope or
goal, so look for links between past associations
and your present dream. Sayings, proverbs and
superstitions can all be associations that are
played out in dreams. For example, you may
dream of too many cooks spoiling the broth,
suggesting that in waking life you feel that too
many people are interfering in your life. Names
and song titles are also good ammunition for
your dreaming mind to convey a message. What
qualities or people do you associate with certain
names? If a song is running through your head
when you wake up try to remember the words as
the message may well be there.

Try to associate your dream with what is
happening in your life now. Are you worried
about an exam, someone you love or a distressing
family situation? Are you looking for someone,

seeking an opportunity or have you just had a fall
out with your best friend? Try to keep in your
mind what is happening in your life and jot down
your thoughts about it.

Having recorded all the different
aspects of your dream you will have
transformed your dream into words
and created a permanent reminder.
No matter how silly it seemed as you wrote it
down you are now ready to try and figure out
what your dream means. Later in the day you
may decide to write out your dream in more
detail but don't leave it too long as the dream
memory will fade. Don't take it too seriously
though. The most important thing is that you
relax, have fun and learn some new things
about yourself from your dreams.

To give you a better idea of how to record your
dreams, here's a sample from a dream diary:

⋆ ⋋ CAROLINE'S DREAM JOURNAL

Dream 46
Date: Sunday 19 August 2005
Time: between 2 and 3 am
Feeling/atmosphere: anxious
Theme: chess game
Movement: train journey
Colours, conversation, sound: dark, no conversation, rain on window
Previous association: Under 16 chess champion in my class at school
Dream title: Chess game
Message: Feeling left out and as if all my friends have a more exciting life than I do.
Details: I was travelling on a train, a very fast train. I had no idea where I was going and didn't seem to be interested. It was late in the evening and was getting dark and I could hear rain on the window. Although the train was packed no-one was speaking. All our attention was on two people playing a game of chess and it was clear that high stakes were involved. On waking I felt very anxious.

✴ PROGRAMMING YOUR MIND FOR DREAM RECALL

Some dreams are so vivid you can't forget them but many are so fleeting they can vanish without a trace. One way to make sure you remember them is to talk to yourself in a positive way. Before going to sleep tell yourself that you will remember your dreams on waking. Try this visualization technique.

When you feel sleepy, turn off the lights and settle down in your favourite sleeping position. In a relaxed way think about what you want to dream. Breathe in for a count of five and out for a count of ten. Repeat this and then breathe normally. Now imagine you have just woken up in the morning, and as you do you reach for your pen and write down your dream. Bring your attention to the present again and feel comfortable and warm and sleepy. Tell yourself that in the morning you will remember your dreams.

With practice, you will soon get the hang of writing down your dreams and unlocking their meaning. If you get stuck with your images and symbols or just want reminding use the Dream Dictionary in chapter nine. Don't forget, though, the best book you will ever read about dreams is the one you write yourself.

CHAPTER FIVE

Dream power

So how can dreams be of use to you in your daily life? How can something that isn't 'real' help you face problems, make decisions and deal with life?

The answer lies with you again. You can take charge of your dreams and turn them into creative and helpful experiences or use them for specific purposes. From now on, stop thinking of your dreams as something random and start thinking about what you want to dream, what you want your dream to resolve and what question you want answered. To do this you have to get your waking mind to work more fully with your dreaming mind. This is a process called dream incubation. It takes some practice but once you get the hang of it you'll be amazed by the power and magic of your dreams to transform your life.

✦✦

Step-by-step guide to dream incubation

Step 1: Decide what you want to dream about, what you want your dream to resolve or help you with and what question you want answered.

Step 2: Write down your question or desired dream on a piece of paper as if you were chatting to a friend – because that's what your dream self is. Be as specific as you can, but don't ask about silly or trivial matters, such as whether you should go shopping or to the cinema with your friend.

Step 3: Read this over and over again during the day and keep it in your mind all day and again as you get ready for bed. (By the way it's not a good idea to do this exercise after watching a late night movie.)

Step 4: Once in bed read over the question again and ask your dreaming self to bring you the answer during sleep. Put the paper under your pillow or near your bed.

Step 5: Tell yourself before you go to sleep that you will have the dream you want and trust yourself to dream the dream that you ask for.

Step 6: Be prepared to write down the dream when you wake up and be open to whatever comes to you.

Step 7: Tell yourself you will remember your dream.

Step 8: Relax and leave your dream intention to incubate. What you are doing here is programming your dreaming self – giving it a particular task to focus on.

Step 9: Be willing to experiment and try again if necessary.

You may not want to ask your dreaming self a question and may simply want a happy, harmonious dream. If this is the case think of a place or person you'd like to dream about – perhaps a holiday or Brad Pitt – write down a simple description and ask your dreaming self in the same way to give you a happy dream.

⋆ ⅄ IMAGINE, IMAGINE, IMAGINE

In the following chapters you'll discover how to use dream power to help you with various aspects of your life from love and relationships, to friends, school and future career choices. Just bear in mind before you begin your dream work that when it comes to fulfilling your dreams and hopes for the future your greatest gift is your imagination. When you imagine something you create a picture of it in your mind and if you use the dream incubation step-by-step technique to reflect this in a dream it can help you realize the dream in your waking life. Although there is no guarantee that this will always happen your imagination has set everything in motion. If you start with good intent (you are unlikely to get what you want in life if you are selfish, flippant or greedy) and set up the structure through which things can happen (if you want to be a doctor you also need to work hard and get into medical school) the chances of it happening in real life are very good indeed. Every success and goal achieved in life starts with imagination. Why not use yours to help make your dreams come true?

✲✶ DAYDREAMING

Have you ever daydreamed in a 'what if' kind of way? Daydreaming has an important place in helping dreams come true. When you relax and let your mind wonder you are tapping into your inner inspiration because you are imagining all sorts of possibilities for yourself.

✲✶ LUCID DREAMING

Lucid dreaming is when you are dreaming but know you are dreaming. It's like you create the dream scene or take part in the action and decide what's going to happen. Not everyone has lucid dreams but the fact that many people do shows that dreams can be controlled. It shows that you

do have choices in life and that you are the
person in charge – even while you sleep.

You are more likely to experience a lucid
dream when you are in a light sleep – for
example, when you have dozed off after your
alarm clock has gone or when you nap in the day.
If you do take a nap during the day you might
like to tell your dreaming mind to go into lucid
dreaming mode, as there is a problem you need
to sort out or something that you want to
understand better. As you drift in and out of
sleep keep thinking of this.

What may happen is that you start to dream
and then you think you have woken up but you
haven't – you are still in a dream state. It's now
that you can take control. Try to set the scene,
talk to the people you need to or ask for help to
find solutions. When you do finally wake up you
may wonder if you really are awake so give
yourself time to ponder what your dreaming
self has discovered.

*⅄ DREAM MAGIC

Whether you experience lucid dreams or not, any dream you have has the potential to take you to a world of mystery and wonder that can keep you spellbound for days. In all this never forget that you are the dreamer and by understanding your dreams you will reach a better understanding of yourself. Relax and enjoy the drama, excitement and magic each and every dream brings.

Don't let yourself get so caught up, though, that you can't tell what's real and what's a dream. Remember that your everyday life is what is important – contact with real people, real situations and actual happenings. Keeping a sense of perspective and being level-headed counts for a great deal. For your dream life to be rich and magical you need to live your life to the full.

CHAPTER SIX

Love and relationships

Your dreams can give you a great insight into many areas of your life. Relationships are a major part of your life. You can put your dreams to use in relationships of all kinds: with your parents, brothers, sisters, teachers, relatives, friends and, of course, your boyfriend or someone you are interested in romantically.

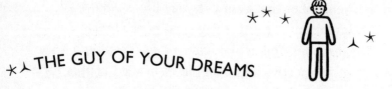

THE GUY OF YOUR DREAMS

If you haven't got a boyfriend and want to visualize the perfect boy for you, you can use the following as a guideline.

Close your eyes and take a few deep breaths. Imagine the guy of your dreams standing in front of you. When you have a clear vision and feel calm and ready, tell yourself that you are worthy of love. Ask your dreams to help you find the guy of your dreams in waking life.

It's important that you have a really clear image of the kind of boy you want in your life and also a strong sense of self-worth. You deserve the best and you'll settle for nothing less. It might help to actually write down a description of your perfect partner. Focus not on appearance but on the qualities you desire. Ask your dreaming self to help you in your quest for love and place your dream intention under your pillow. As you dream you may get some advice or even have visions of future happiness. If that doesn't happen, don't worry, your dreaming self may simply be reminding you that right now there are other things in life, such as schoolwork, outside interests and friends, that require your attention first. Remember your dreaming self always has your best interests at heart.

If you have a boyfriend but things aren't going too well, think about what makes you feel good about the relationship and what doesn't make you feel so good. Then think about how you'd like things to be. Now ask your dreaming self to give you guidance and advice.

✶⋏ LOVE

Dreams of love are often thought provoking. Have you ever woken from a dream in tears because it touched you so deeply? You may feel a brief but intense heartbreak when you realize that the guy who swept you off your feet existed only in dreamland.

Dreams with romantic themes try to answer questions you may have about love. This is no small order and in the search for answers your dreaming mind will scan past relationships, try on celebrities and friends as boyfriends and show you how things might or might not work out.

There is a part of ourselves that is always thinking about love and trying to figure out how things can work or work better. Love is important to us all and that's why we have so many dreams about it. Your dreaming self is always trying to generate ideas and give you warnings.

You'll probably recognize a 'love me, love me not' storyline in your dreams. Why? Because your dreaming self is trying to help you figure out how to win love. In your dream you may be thrown together with someone you fancy. When you wake up the question then becomes, have you got a crush on this person, or is that person interested in you? You may feel a bit awkward if you bump into that person the next day. You may even be hopeful that your dream revealed a well-concealed interest on their part. Unfortunately this isn't always the case. Sometimes your dreaming self can tune into the feelings of someone you like and try to get the point across in a dream. In other cases these dreams are expressions of your own needs and have nothing to do with the guy you think is really cool. Your dreaming mind tends to test out lots of guys you know so that when the real thing comes along you know how to handle the situation better.

But how can you tell if the guy of your dreams is meant for you? Ask yourself these questions to decide what the odds are that your dream guy is also dreaming of you:

Is he going out with someone else?

⭐ If the answer is yes, then your dream probably has nothing to do with his feelings at all. Enjoy the experience and focus your attention on someone who is available.

Does he seem interested in you in real life?

⭐ If the answer is yes, your dream might be giving you a hint. If no, don't chase him because of your dream. The fact that you are having romantic dreams and trying out different guys shows that your romantic radar is working well.

Are you already going out with someone?

⭐ Strangely enough romantic dreams about other people have more to do with the relationship you are in than they do with fantasy encounters. Your dream may highlight qualities you would like more of in your current relationship so don't make the mistake of thinking there is something wrong with your boyfriend. Dreams often try to help define what you need and want so that you can develop these with the love you already have. On the other hand, if you find that you really aren't happy with your boyfriend then insisting on something that isn't working will just block the right person from finding you. Let go and trust that a positive, hopeful attitude will attract the guy of your dreams to you.

Why would I dream of someone I'm not attracted to?

★ There are times when we feel a spark of an attraction to someone but by day it is well concealed for one reason or another. But if you honestly don't find the other person attractive then there may be another explanation. That person could represent a quality or characteristic of your own personality that you need to develop. For example, a romantic dream about Robin Williams could represent a need to cultivate your sense of humour; or an encounter with Jonathon

Ross could symbolize the need for better communication skills. If, however, your dream guy is particularly unsavoury and you get a real sense of loathing, you need to make a mental note of what specific characteristics made them so. Then you need to think about what activity or person in your life makes you feel this way. It could be time to reevaluate your choices and be willing to say no if something isn't right for you.

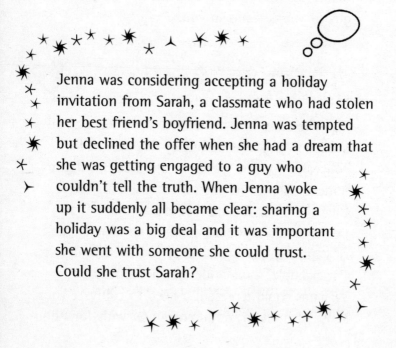

Jenna was considering accepting a holiday invitation from Sarah, a classmate who had stolen her best friend's boyfriend. Jenna was tempted but declined the offer when she had a dream that she was getting engaged to a guy who couldn't tell the truth. When Jenna woke up it suddenly all became clear: sharing a holiday was a big deal and it was important she went with someone she could trust. Could she trust Sarah?

Another way to interpret dreams about unsuitable partners is to think if you are connecting with the person you dreamt about in way that isn't romantic. For example, you may dream about a boy in your class who is assigned to be your partner in a debate. You don't find that boy attractive but you make an excellent debating team.

What if I dream I am a member of the opposite sex?

⭐ This kind of dream can be a bit of a shocker but in most cases gender shifting dreams deal with exploring different aspects of yourself, such as your masculine qualities. Don't judge yourself harshly if you have these kinds of dreams. We all have them and they appear to be markers of maturity more than anything else.

Dreams when inappropriate relationships, for example with a family member, are played out can also be shocking. Fortunately most dreams of this type are symbolic. You could be involved with someone who reminds you of a relative or they can symbolize love that is too close, too enmeshed and confused. In other words, you could be picking up on something that is unwholesome about a current relationship.

Are dreams of a guy two-timing me warning signs of real trouble?

⭐ Some are but for the most part dreams about your boyfriend two-timing or chatting up another girl are not indicators of actual cheating. Instead these dreams often suggest that your boyfriend could be giving his mates more time and attention than you.

Dreams about ex-boyfriends

⭐ Relax, dreams about ex-boyfriends don't necessarily mean that you want to be with them again. Dreams like this occur to both heal and help you assimilate new experiences. They are your way of getting over past relationships, so don't feel you are failing when they crop up. It can take time for emotional wounds to heal and you may continue to have dreams of ex-boyfriends even when you have moved on. Accept them and realize your deeper mind is working hard to move you forward to a positive present. If you haven't got another boyfriend your dreaming mind will sometimes create scenarios using your past love experiences to try and make sense of what will work for you in the future. You are, in a sense, getting ready to love more successfully next time. The dreams that are setting the stage for this to happen just use your ex as the actor who represents the love interest. He will appear and you may have all kinds of adventures as your mind unravels mistakes and gains understanding about the things that make real love work.

What if you have a boyfriend and dream you kiss someone else?

⋆ Dreams in which you get close to another boy don't usually indicate unhappiness with your current boyfriend. Your dreaming self is just sorting through what works and doesn't work in a relationship and will refer back to past loves or create new ones to compare strengths and weaknesses or make sense of patterns.

Is there any hope of meeting the guy of my dreams in real life?

☆ Surprisingly yes. If you do have a perfect romantic dream it may be your intuition warming you up or reminding you that love does lie ahead for you. However, don't run off with the first person you see the next day, but do open yourself up to the possibility that a romance may be on the horizon.

★★★

Interpreting romantic dreams

Romantic dreams, like their real life counterparts, are fraught with emotion and desire. You awake from them aroused, excited, sad and confused. You may even feel ashamed or embarrassed about the dream you had and it can be hard to discuss such dreams with your friends for fear of being teased. When dreams of a delicate subject matter happen and you don't feel you can talk to anyone you can refer to the following list to see if you can relate to certain aspects.

✴⅄ COMMON LOVE DREAMS

In my dream I spent the whole time searching for a place to be alone with my boyfriend but couldn't find one.

This isn't really a dream about love but about trying to communicate with someone important to you and feeling frustrated that the opportunity doesn't seem to be presenting itself.

✳ ✳

We were walking down the high street holding hands and kissing and the head teacher walks by. He stopped us and asked us about our homework.

Dreams of interrupted intimacy suggest that there are outside forces intruding on your relationship or yourself. Perhaps parents and teachers have opinions and expectations that are stifling.

Would you believe it? We were kissing and it was on television all over the world!

Dreams like this suggest that you feel you and your boyfriend are very much in the public eye.

✳ ✳

I ran into the arms of my boyfriend. Then he vanished.

Once again this type of dream suggests a need for greater connection and closeness, not just with your boyfriend but with your family and friends too.

✳ ✳

I had a wonderful date but he had no face.

This kind of dream is a gift because it creates an unforgettable sample of the kind of love out there waiting for you. It lets you know how good you will feel when you meet that special guy.

✳ ✳

Things to remember ...

1. Don't judge the dream by how you feel when you wake up. Disapproval and fear won't help you make sense of the dream.

2. Consider what the dream has to tell you about love and romance. Does it help you see things from a different point of view or through someone else's eyes?

3. Don't feel guilty. Now you know that your dreams use images and symbols you don't need to feel ashamed. See these dreams as opportunities to learn about yourself.

4. Be tactful and respectful of the feelings of others. It is not a good idea to tell your boyfriend you have been dreaming about his best mate, for example!

5. Above all, trust your dreams and think positively. However strange, your dream will always have an underlying positive message. There is a lesson, an insight or something healing and inspiring being offered, so make sure you are open to these possibilities.

CHAPTER SEVEN

Health, friends, family, school and work

Even though it might seem like it at times, boys aren't the only important things in your busy life. Nothing is more important than your health, for example. Then there are your friends and family, school, outside interests and, of course, your future career. Your dreaming mind, registering how significant all these are for your general well-being, will continually process information and sort through ideas in your dreams to improve your understanding.

Your health

Just as sleep heals your body and mind, your dreams can use mental imagery that can help you change or adjust your behaviour, habits and lifestyle to keep you healthy.

Your body does speak to you in other ways than through pain and you may well find that your dreams reflect a state of poor health. If you wake up from a dream with a sense of rottenness or decay, or if you eat rotten food or see flowers withering in a dream, the chances are you may not be paying enough attention to your health. Do a quick review of your eating and lifestyle habits. Are you doing the best for yourself?

You may also find when you are ill that your dream reflects this. If you have a cold or flu you may dream that you can't breathe. If your chest is sore you may dream of fighting. If you have a fever you may dream of a fire. You may also have a dream which forecasts a physical problem before it happens.

But how can you tell when a dream is a health warning? The key to recognizing your own healing imagery is to be familiar with your own particular dream signs and dream signals. If you have a dream which has unusual imagery which is very different from your usual dream symbols, ask yourself if that dream is health related. For example, if you normally dream of dogs and it is a pleasant experience but then have a scary dream when a dog attacks you in the stomach, this could suggest forthcoming health problems, such as a stomach upset.

Just as our dreams address our hopes and fears about our interactions with other people and the world, they can also help us understand how we feel about ourselves and our physical and emotional health. The mind is just as important as the body in healing and may even take the lead in the healing process. So why not harness your dream's healing potential and take the leap towards a healthier you? More and more evidence suggests that mind over matter is far more than just a truism. My best suggestion is to try it and see.

✗⊁ USING DREAMS TO IMPROVE YOUR GENERAL WELL-BEING

Once again brainstorm by using the following to help you get clear on just how you want your dream to assist you. Then refer to the information on dream incubation on pages 52–53 and make a request to your dream mind.

My self-image...
    My health...
       My exercise routine...
         My eating habits...

Just before you go to sleep ask your dreaming self to give you an answer. Then when you wake up write it down straight away. If it doesn't seem to relate to your health, try again the next night. As you know perseverance is one of the most important aspects of working with dreams and their imagery!

75

Friends and family

Family members, friends from school and your other interests are probably some of the most important elements in your life right now, so it is hardly surprising that they often figure in your dreams.

One theory is that dreams about family and friends represent elements present in your own personality, but in the majority of cases it is easier to understand dreams about friends and family members by accepting that they are just being themselves. Regardless of how strange your dream may seem, when you dream about your friends they are not appearing at random. Each one is deliberately selected by your dreaming self because something about them best captures the kind of energy that is being expressed in the dream.

Laura used to be very close to a girl called Sophie. They trained at dance school together. The girls lost touch when Sophie moved to the States with her parents. Laura often wonders what Sophie is up to and whether or not she has taken her dancing further. One night Laura dreamt that Sophie called her on the telephone and told her she had landed a part in a major Broadway musical. When Laura woke up she felt excited. She had recently applied to dance college and her dream simply made her feel more determined.

When you dream about family members, you have a chance to learn more about their point of view, what motivates them and how your actions may be affecting them. Lisa was unaware of just how cranky she'd become with her Mum until she dreamt of responding to her Mum's suggestion that she tidy up her room by biting her head off!

If you find that in your dreams concerning friends and family there is violence and action, they usually reflect emotional hurts that you need to deal with in waking life. You may also encounter eccentric forms, fancy clothes and other weird pursuits. Don't worry about these too much – your dreams are just trying to find ways to express themselves and sometimes they will reflect more honestly and clearly the feelings you have been struggling with during the day. They can also give you an opportunity to understand another person's viewpoint or to recognize a growing rift.

Caroline was upset because her best friend, Debbie, was subtly turning against her. Instead of shared laughter there was tension and Caroline began to feel that Debbie was taking advantage of her. Caroline had no idea what she had done to upset Debbie. One night she dreamt that Debbie and her were playing a game of squash. At the end of a sweaty game Debbie said: 'Look the reason I can't stand you is because your grades were better than mine and you are going to go to university and meet the man of your dreams. I'm probably not going to get into university and it's killing me.' Caroline awoke feeling stunned but also rather relieved that she had found a possible source of Debbie's unhappiness and frustration. She decided to talk to her friend to find out exactly what was upsetting her and try to work things out.

When dreaming about friends, what they say and do is key to the meaning of your dream. They will show you how in real life you see your place in the group or family. Good friends are supportive and affectionate, and to experience a happy dream in their company is probably a sign that things are currently going well in your life. A dream when you row, fight or disagree shows that you or they are feeling angry or disappointed in some way. Dreams about family, on the other hand, will tend to reflect something about your attitudes to family life – perhaps an issue to do with family meal times or curfews. Through the feelings and behaviour in the dream you may see a family member in a different light or gain a new understanding about your own role in the family.

When dreaming about friends and family try to focus on your sense of what they represent. This is especially important when your dreams seem illogical or hard to interpret. That way you'll understand more about your genuine reactions to life and the motivations and agendas of those around you. When you start to do this you'll find that your close relationships become much easier to understand and enjoy.

Always remember that however helpful your dreams, talking to your friends and family is the best way to solve problems, sort differences and see a way forward. Though your dreams can give you a great insight into your relationships they cannot replace face-to-face communication.

School

You may dream about school if you are going through tough times with your friends, teachers or work, especially if something in real life has upset you. This type of dream is really a means by which your dreaming self can express your feelings and bring things to your attention – perhaps something you have said that was important but you didn't catch.

Generally though, dreams about school tell you there's something important you need to learn, and that life is or may be about to teach you that lesson. It's vital then, to identify this in (not with) your waking life, for it could be a message from your inner self. On another level, it could simply suggest that you need to seek information about someone you know or a project you are working on. Have you got all the facts or do you need to dig deeper?

✱⅄ INCUBATING A DREAM TO HELP WITH SCHOOLWORK

If you want your dreams to help you make positive changes in your schoolwork think about what changes you would like to make. Could you ask your teacher for more help? Spend more time on your homework? Get down to your homework before you switch on the television? Hang out with your friends after you have finished your studies?

When you are clear about how you want your dreams to assist you, you will know how to word your request to your dreaming mind. If you are anxious about a particular subject or assignment

 prepare by asking your teacher for guidance and get all the help and information you can. Do searches on the Internet and read books on the topic. The more involved you are with a subject the more help you will get when you call upon your dream mind for assistance.

Work

So what do you want to do with the rest of your life? If you haven't got a clue you can use your dreams to point you in the right direction. Kelly finds that whenever she dreams about travel she wakes up feeling happy and excited. Kelly isn't quite sure what she wants to do but one thing her dreams have helped her realize is that she can't work in an office. She needs to think about work that keeps her on the move.

On the other hand, if you know exactly what you want to do dreams can help you with any problems, ideas and questions you might have. Alice is determined to be a doctor but isn't sure how to go about it. In one particular dream she found herself working in a busy hospital. People kept asking her for directions but she didn't know the answer. Each time she told them to talk to the person in charge. Alice's dream is urging her to seek advice from someone in authority, such as a parent or a teacher.

Your dreams can help you with concerns and questions that you might have because they help you tap into your creativity, which can guide you towards the right career choice for you.

 There are three stages in the creative process. The first stage is information gathering, when you research the idea, think about solutions and brainstorm with others. So if you don't know what you want to do with your life take some time to explore the wonderful options that are out there. It is often at the end of this stage that we say we will 'sleep on it' because we haven't yet arrived at a solution.

The second stage is where dreaming comes in. It's in this stage that you appear to give up. But in reality you have sent the question to your dreaming mind to work on. Then the final stage is that 'ahh' moment when the way forward becomes clearer and there is less confusion. For instance, you have been thinking about teaching as a career but your real passion is music. In your dream you see yourself teaching music and realize that becoming a teacher doesn't mean you have to give up your passion.

To get the most out of your dreams so that they can help you face everyday problems and questions it helps to be creative. But don't panic if you don't think you are – creative skills can be acquired. What traits are common to creative people?

✧ The ability to listen to others without judging.

✧ The ability to listen to your heart.

✧ The ability to think outside the box.

Not sure what all this means? Here's a simple way to test your creativity.

Think of a cardboard box. It's a magic box that can do or become anything. Without giving it any thought list ten potential uses of that box on a piece of paper. So what did you do with your box? I'm sure your ideas were wonderfully creative. Now all you need to do is apply that same skill to your dreams. Creative dreams can help you see things from a different perspective, notice things that you might have missed and try out different solutions. What they

won't do is make your decisions for you. It's up to
you to listen to what your dreams have to say and
then listen to your heart and head.

Creative dreaming really is simple, so give it a
try. The only barriers seem to be if you are tired or
if you are trying too hard. Ask your dreaming
mind to help you answer questions relating to life,
school and work by following the dream
incubation guidelines on pages 52–53. Let your
dreams help you expand your vision and see a
way forward. The possibilities for the rest of your
life are limited only when you don't take
advantage of your greatest resource of all –
your imagination.

CHAPTER EIGHT

Fears and hopes

Fears

Being attacked, chased or other scary happenings in dreams can leave you feeling pretty jittery for hours, sometimes days, after the dream has occurred. Why do we have disturbing dreams? What are they telling us about our waking life? Disturbing dreams reflect anxiety, both great and small, that is going on in our waking life. Sometimes they occur because we are going through a major trauma, such as parents splitting up or the death of a loved one, and sometimes they occur because of minor upsets, such as falling out with friends or losing a purse. But disturbing dreams can also occur when our lives seem to be anxiety-free. When this happens you need to examine the dream pictures very closely – never forget that these pictures come from your own mind.

✶⅄ SOMETHING IN THE BEDROOM

One of the most common dreams for young people is that there is something scary in the bedroom. There may be a monster in the closet, something sinister under the bed, bogeymen in the corner of the room, or just something horrible coming to get you.

Dreams like this are often the result of feelings of uncertainty, inconsistency and a lack of control over your circumstances. Perhaps a new sibling has arrived on the scene or there is friction among your parents. Generally creatures or horrible things tend to represent situations. Monsters, on the other hand, tend to represent people.

*⅄ MONSTERS

It's very likely that you have dreamt about monsters. Some may bear a striking resemblance to adults you know. Witches can sometimes represent aspects of your Mum that have created conflict. But this doesn't mean you hate your Mum or are afraid of her. Monster dreams reveal the scary side of adults and this can be quite frightening. Think about it. Have you ever seen a teacher or a friend get really cross when they were stressed or tired? You probably learned to not talk to them until they got back to their normal selves. In other words you learned to tread wearily. It can be quite frightening when Mum is replaced by the scary witch or parents become shouting monsters arguing in the front seat of a car. Well, your dream monsters reflect the tension and show how frightening it is when people we trust behave strangely. Even fairly harmless things can also trigger strong reactions, such as the eccentric uncle whose glass eye alarms you or the spooky neighbour with a high pitched voice.

✳⅄ WILD ANIMAL ATTACK

Snapping dogs, alligators, wild bears and lions are among the most common examples of wild animals in dreams, and they tend to be linked to particular situations or people that trouble you. For instance, Ella dreamt of a mean bull chasing her night after night during the term she was assigned to a really strict maths teacher who put lots of pressure on her. Tori dreamt of a wild lion chasing her in the woods and she knew she had to outwit the animal or it would kill her. At the time her parents were in financial trouble and the dream reflected her feeling of being in a situation that needed her to cut down on unnecessary expenses and handle her pocket money more carefully.

✗⅄ SOMETHING ORDINARY TURNS SINISTER

Dreams when something harmless, like a toy or a musical instrument, turns menacing and starts to chase you, can reflect tensions about normal situations that make you feel anxious. For example, your grandparents come to stay – a perfectly normal event – but the tension between your Mum and her in-laws makes you feel uneasy.

✗⅄ SINISTER, REPETITIVE TASK

In this kind of dream a repetitive task must be performed usually at the command of monsters. The task may be something horrendous like digging graves or sorting body parts. The dreamer is numb to the horror by the sheer boredom and repetition of the task. This kind of dream is very common if you have been successful but feel under constant stress to meet high standards.

Perhaps you have been sacrificing a lot to achieve good exam results and a part of you longs to relax, unwind and have some fun.

BREATHING UNDERWATER

Have you ever had a dream when you were underwater and couldn't breathe, or perhaps you were frozen in place and couldn't move? There is the truly horrifying moment when you know you are going to drown or get hit by an approaching car and then amazingly you learn to breathe underwater or have the strength to move out of the way. This kind of dream suggests a sense of feeling overwhelmed perhaps by school, perhaps by an intense friendship and an inability to express your true feelings. There is a surprise happy ending though indicating that within you is the strength to find solutions to a difficult situation. If your dream doesn't end happily it could simply mean that right now there doesn't seem to be any way out but this isn't to say that you can't find one.

✶⅄ EVIL FORCES

In such dreams you are faced with a terrifying evil force but just when all hope is lost you become a super-heroine with amazing powers. Like the breathing underwater dream this reflects tension and struggle in your life but it also shows you that if you can summon your inner strength you will pull through.

✶⅄ BURYING A DEAD BODY

This dream involves the awareness that you have somehow killed someone and you have to dispose of the body. Despite the horror of this dream your main concern is avoiding discovery. Such a dream is connected with the need for acceptance and the decision to hide things about yourself that you think won't be acceptable. Perhaps you are ashamed of things you used to like and want to put all that behind you.

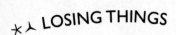 LOSING THINGS

When we forget or lose things in dreams this
tends to represent our identity. For example,
Michelle had a dream that she lost her bag when
she was out to lunch with her friends. Less than a
week before her boyfriend had told her he didn't
want to see her anymore. Even though she felt
she was coping okay the dream reflected her fear
of making her way without him.

DEATH OF A PARENT

Your chief concern if you have a dream like this is
that it may be foreshadowing a real event. It isn't.
It simply means that you are growing up, moving
towards your adult self and redefining your
relationship with your parents.

★⅄ UNDERSTANDING NIGHTMARES

Everyone has nightmares and they usually reflect fears or situations in our lives that frighten us. But, like all dreams, they occur to help us deal with waking issues by presenting difficult situations in a new light. If you have a scary dream have a think about what is going on in your life at the moment. How you regard your dreams, even the frightening ones, says a lot about your approach to issues in your waking life. It's up to you now. Are you going to do something about the situation that is unsettling you? If you feel you can't do anything are you going to ask for help?

Hopes

We all have hopes and dreams – they are part of what makes up amazing you. What are yours? Why not use your dreaming mind to help make your wishes come true. Remember when it comes

to wish fulfilment your greatest asset is
your imagination. You imagine something
– you create a picture of it in your mind –
and using the dream incubation technique you
learned about on pages 52–53 you instruct your
dreaming self to reflect this wish in a dream and
help you live the dream when you are awake. For
example, if you want to do well at school and end
the year on a high with the coolest birthday
party ever, start thinking, dreaming and
working towards that today. In other words,
let your imagination and your dreams help
you create what you want in your waking life. You
may not believe it but dreams have a habit of
coming true so be careful and concise with your
instructions to your dream self.

The more you work with your dreams the
more you will begin to understand them, and the
more you appreciate them the more you will
understand yourself. Understanding yourself is
crucial for success and happiness in life because
you come to know your strengths and weaknesses.

You know that you have choices in life and that you are in charge and can find a way to achieve the best outcome. Armed with the confidence that only self-knowledge can bring, you really do have all that you need to make your dreams come true.

CHAPTER NINE

Your dream dictionary

It won't take you long to get the hang of dream interpretation. If you want a little help you can use this Dream Dictionary to prompt your memory. Remember though that dreams are unique and individual so any guide can never be totally correct and the best dream dictionary for you is the one that you write yourself with the free association method discussed in chapter three (see pages 30–34). This guide is here to help you question and consider more deeply the likely significance of some of the most typical dream elements so that you can draw your own conclusions about what your dreaming self or inner wisdom is trying to tell you.

For example, say you dream of a snake. First of all think about all the feelings that your snake dream left you with. Do you feel anxious, calm or angry? Then have a think about how you feel about snakes. Are you frightened of snakes, fascinated or indifferent? Then think about all the things you might associate a snake with: the serpent in the Biblical story of Adam and Eve, for example, or perhaps something you know about snakes, like they shed their skins or some strangle their victims. When you have done all that come back to your dream and work out what your dream is trying to tell you. Perhaps the snake in your dream is urging you to leave old habits behind and start afresh; maybe the snake is warning you about an untrustworthy friend; or perhaps you have been a little disobedient recently?

You'll know when you hit the right interpretation because you'll get that 'ahh' feeling when everything just makes sense. If you don't get the 'ahh' feeling write down your dream and keep thinking about your dream snake image during the day. The chances are you'll have another dream the next night that will help explain and clarify, and if that doesn't happen maybe you'll get clarity in a few weeks, months or even years when you re-read your dream journal and everything falls into place. Remember sometimes you need the perspective of time to see how all the pieces of your life fit together.

Look up your dream images here and see what you can discover about your dreams!

Dream Dictionary

Accidents: Do you need to take more care or watch out for mistakes? Is something in your life out of control?

Aeroplane: Do you need to get away from it all? Is it time to try something new? Is it time to get another person's point of view about something? Do you need to come down to earth and face reality?

Aliens: Are you currently in a place or situation that you don't understand or with which you feel very uncomfortable? Do you feel isolated and confused?

Alleyways: Is there light at the end of the tunnel? Are you lost? Do you call out for help? Do you need to ask someone for advice in waking life?

Amusement arcades: Is it time to keep playing or is it time to quit while you are ahead?

Angels: Are you waiting for news about something or someone? Are you looking for answers? Angels are symbols of love and happiness so your answer could be much closer than you think.

Animals: Animals in dreams reflect basic reactions and instincts. What feelings did you experience in the dream? Do you recognize yourself or someone you know in the animal?

Avalanche: Are you feeling overwhelmed by school-work? Can you find ways to reduce your workload?

Babies: Do you have hidden talents just waiting to be discovered?

Bags: All kinds of luggage tend to be associated with responsibilities. Is the baggage yours or someone else's? Do you feel burdened? Did you off-load or dump your bag? What was in the bag?

Balls: Are you playing in a team or on your own? How well are you getting on with your friends and family right now?

Beach: Do you feel really relaxed or do you long to get away from it all?

Bees: Do you have a bee in your bonnet about something or someone? Are you busy like a bee? Were you stung in your dream? Has someone let you down?

Bells: Are you expecting news about someone or something?

Boats: Any moving vessel in a dream represents the progress you are making in life. Is it plain sailing and are you on course? Or are conditions rough?

Boyfriend: Do you need to feel loved?

Candles: Candles are symbols of wisdom and understanding. Is your candle bright or is it flickering?

Cars: In whatever way a car appears in a dream it tends to represent your energy, ambition or the way you do things. Are you running smoothly or stop-starting? Are you in the driver's seat or is the car out of your control?

Castles: Are your plans realistic?

Cats: Are you listening to your intuition? Is there someone in your life that you shouldn't trust? Are you feeling lucky?

Chased: What are you trying to avoid? Do you need to cut to the chase and take swift action?

Classroom: Classrooms often symbolize a part of ourselves, and the action there describes what is happening to us and how we are feeling.

Climbing: Climbing often symbolizes ambition. Are you climbing with ease or is progress tough? Are you climbing up or down?

Colours: Colours have their own special descriptive language in dreams. The following associations might help you work out their meaning in your dream:

Black: Are things negative at the moment, or is a time of rest called for before the next phase begins?

Blue: How are your communication skills? Do you feel calm? Or do you have the blues?

Gold: Have you reached a rewarding phase in your life?

Green: Do you feel hopeful right now or do you have a lot to learn?

Orange: Do you like to be the centre of attention? Are you feeling energetic?

Pink: Are you feeling happy and healthy?

Purple: Are you being oversensitive or not being sensitive enough? Is it time to step back and see things in perspective?

Red: Are you in love or are you very angry? Would you like to paint the town red?

Silver: Do you need to use your intuition more? Or is it time to see things more realistically?

White: Is it time for a fresh start?

Yellow: Are you feeling creative? Or do you associate this colour with spineless behaviour?

Computers: Do you need to apply logic to a situation? Is it time to increase your knowledge with application?

Crocodiles: How do you view crocodiles and alligators in waking life?

Crying: Is there a sense of loss that you haven't come to terms with?

Death: Is this the end of a phase and the beginning of another for you? For example, leaving school or home, or starting a new relationship?

Diamonds: Diamonds are symbols of truth and beauty. Should you look at all aspects of a situation just as a cut diamond has many facets? How brilliant is your stone? Are you given it or do you find it yourself?

Dieting: Is food or losing weight on your mind? Do you need to budget more and cut out unnecessary extravagance?

Doctor: Do you long to be looked after or do you need to be more caring towards someone?

Dogs: Loyalty, friendship and trust are the key words for dogs. How do you generally feel about dogs in your waking life?

Dolphins: Dolphins are symbols of healing, joy and intelligence. Do you need to sharpen up or lighten up?

Doors: Is the door open or closed? What kind of a door is it? Are you ready to go through to the next phase of your development?

Doves: Doves are symbols of peace, hope, love and calm. Is this what you need in your life right now?

Drowning: Do you need to come up for air?

Eagles: Do you long to soar above the rest? Do you need to use your eagle eye in waking life?

Eating: Is life a bit dull and do you need the taste of new experiences? Do you need to chew things over? Do you need to cooperate more with others?

Embarrassment: Do you feel vulnerable and lacking in self-confidence?

Escaping: Do you long to break free? Do you need to take control or release yourself from a situation?

Exams: Are you worried about looking foolish? Are you finding it hard to stick to the rules set by other people? Does your dream relate to a real life exam or testing times in your life?

Eyes: Are your eyes wide open or closed? Are you seeing situations clearly?

Falling: Do you feel out of control? Does life seem unstable at present? Are you in love? Do you feel on shaky ground about a decision you need to make? If so, seek advice from an adult you can trust.

Fame: Do you need more recognition in your waking life?

Family: Is this about loyalty or unity? Is it time to put your attitude about family life under the spotlight?

Famous people: Do you feel star struck or chosen? What qualities does the person have that you admire? Do you have a secret desire to be recognized by others?

Fashion: Is this all about your self-image? Are you worrying too much about what others think of you?

Father: How well you get on with or know your father in real life affects how you understand what your dream is reflecting. How does this father image appear in your dream? Is it your own father or someone else's?

Fences: Do you feel fenced in? Are you being stopped from doing something you want to do in your waking life? Do you look over the fence to see what is on the other side?

Fighting: Are you struggling with anger or frustration or do you need to fight your corner?

Fire: Does your dream relate to your heartfelt emotions? Are you angry about something or with someone?

Flying: Have you overcome any difficulties recently? Have you experienced success and risen above problems? Do you feel as if you have been released from limitations imposed upon you?

Friends: How do you see your place in the group? What your friends do and say in your dream will be key to its meaning. Do you feel let down, disappointed or happy?

Gardens: Gardens are usually associated with peace, beauty and fragrance but much depends on the state of your garden. Is your garden overgrown? Does something or someone, perhaps yourself, in real life need your attention or care?

Gender reversal: Dreams of this kind are nature's way of releasing tension. They are very common and very healthy. If you dream of being a boy when you are a girl perhaps you need to recognize the so-called masculine qualities of assertiveness and initiating action.

Ghosts: Are you being forced to do something you disapprove of?

Gifts: Is the gift pleasant or unpleasant? Are your talents being recognized or are you undervaluing yourself?

Graves: Do you feel lonely or isolated in waking life or do you want to bury the past or end a real life relationship?

Gun: Who is holding the gun? Gunfire acts as a warning. Do you feel nervous but want to change a situation in your life?

Hair: Are you combing your hair? Could you be about to untangle a problem? Are you having your hair cut? Are you starting something new? Are you cutting someone else's hair? Do you have hidden jealousies? Is your hair falling out? Are you worrying about something?

Hands: Are you frightened of making mistakes? Are you losing your touch or finding things hard to handle?

Horses: Horses are symbols of strength, speed, grace and wisdom. How do you feel about horses in waking life? How do you feel about your progress in life?

Hospital: Are you feeling run down? Do you need to take better care of yourself?

Houses: Do you dream of finding new rooms? Houses represent you the dreamer and the rooms all the different aspects of your personality, so are you uncovering new aspects of yourself in waking life?

Illness: Is your health okay? Have you been overdoing it?

Insects: Do you feel irritated or annoyed by petty issues in your life? Is something or someone bugging you?

Invisibility: Do you feel ignored? Do you sometimes feel insignificant? Do you want to hide? Has there been a lot of change recently in your life?

Islands: Do you feel isolated? Do you long to get away from it all? Do you want to be rescued?

Jewellery: How do you feel about yourself? Is the jewellery flashy or precious and rare? Is your dream about a ring? Do you long for continuity and stability in your life?

Journeys: Do you feel that you are losing your way? Life is a journey and journeys often represent your progress. How are you travelling? Is your journey fast, slow, crowded or difficult? Have you missed a connection? Are you travelling alone?

Jugglers: Jugglers often reflect your abilities and coping skills. Are you keeping all the balls in the air?

Keyhole: Do you have an insight into a situation that no-one else has? Are you being spied on? Are you prying into other people's affairs?

Keys: Do you need to open up to new possibilities?

Killing: Have you been watching too many late night movies? Is a phase in your life coming to an end or are you about to begin something new?

Kissing: Is the kiss enjoyable and sincere or is it meaningless and disappointing? Focus on the way you feel about the kiss here rather than the kiss itself. Do you long for approval? Also remember the saying, 'kiss and tell'. Is someone betraying you?

Knots: Is there a complex situation in your life that needs to be untangled? Are you tying up loose ends in your dream?

Ladder: Are you going up in the world or are you finding it difficult?

Legs: Are you standing up for yourself? Do you feel out of control or that you haven't got a leg to stand on? Or do you feel that you are rising in status? Are your legs heavy and you can't run? Do you need to do something you would rather not do?

Letters: What does your letter say? Is exciting news on its way?

Library: A library in a dream is a symbol of knowledge. What state is your library in?

Light: Is something being illuminated or made clear to you? What colour is your light?

Lions: Lions are symbols of strength and courage. Are you brave or do you need to be strong? Is someone making you feel anxious?

Loss of belongings: Have you been true to yourself lately? Do you feel that you don't belong? Have you lost someone through a disagreement?

Make-up: Do you want to change your image in real life? Are you hiding behind a mask and not showing your true feelings?

Marriage: Who is getting married? Are you thinking a lot about relationships or working with someone else on a project?

Money: Money can represent self-worth so how did you feel about spending money in your dream? What was the money made of?

Moon: Are you using your intuition and feelings before you make decisions?

Mother: Do you feel the need to be looked after or have you started to mother someone or something in your life?

Music: Are you working to your full potential? Perhaps you have hidden talents?

Nails: Is progress slow for you right now? Do you feel under pressure to deliver the goods?

Naked: If you are naked this could mean that you feel vulnerable and exposed. Are you revealing too much about yourself? If you feel at ease this could reflect a sense of self-confidence.

Numbers: Numbers often have special meanings. Try to work out what they mean for you: **1,23**

One is often associated with beginning or your identity.

Two symbolizes duality, special friendships or seeing something from someone else's point of view.

Three is associated with creativity and fun.

Four is associated with self-discipline and responsibility.

Five represents adventure.

Six represents harmony, wisdom and knowledge.

Seven links in with your sensitivity to art, music and literature.

Eight is all about going with the flow.

Nine is associated with caring and sharing.

Ten is all about a job well done and moving forward with confidence to the next stage.

Office: Do you need to be more efficient in your daily life?

Operation: Is there something troubling you? Do you feel vulnerable?

Owls: An owl is symbol of wisdom and mystery. Do you

need to bring these qualities into your life? Or do you need to sharpen your wits?

Parents: How secure do you feel right now? How your parents come across in the dream and how you feel will give you clues to the meaning.

Parties: Are you having fun or feeling left out? What does this say about your social life right now?

Pigs: Have you or someone you know been a little selfish lately?

Police: Do you think you might be caught out doing something you shouldn't? Are you in a situation that could get you into trouble? Or do you thirst for knowledge and authority?

Pregnancy: Has a new project, relationship or phase begun in your life? Have you been waiting a long time for something? Are you developing new skills, new interests, or meeting new people?

Prisons: Are you feeling isolated or trapped?

Prizes: Are you giving yourself enough credit for work well done?

Quarrels: Are you angry with someone? Are you angry with yourself or in conflict about something?

Queen: Is there someone in authority that you look to for advice, a teacher, for instance?

Quicksand: Are you feeling helpless and insecure? Have you got yourself too deep into a situation?

Races: Races usually describe the progress you are making in life. Are you winning or lagging behind?

Rain: Are you feeling refreshed?

Rainbow: Do you feel hopeful and confident again after a difficult patch?

Rats: Do you feel under attack from friends or teachers? Has someone betrayed you?

River: How is the course of your life flowing right now? Is the river calm or turbulent? Is it muddy or clear?

Roads: Roads indicate your journey in life: your past, present and future. Is the road smooth or rough? Is the landscape pretty or rugged?

Roses: Are you in love or passionate about something?

Rubies: Are you feeling passionate and strong about something or someone?

School: Are you going through a difficult time with friends, teachers or work? Is there something you need to learn or pay more attention to? What is happening in the classroom?

Scissors: Do you need to cut out or give up something or someone in

real life? If you are being threatened is someone jealous of you?

Shoes: How do you see yourself and your progress? What condition are your shoes in?

Smells: Is the fragrance sweet or pungent? Is life good right now or is something fishy going on?

Snakes: Have you been disobedient to someone in authority? Is it time to shed your skin and start afresh?

Spiders: Much depends on how you feel about spiders in real life. Do you feel lucky or do you have enemies you need to watch out for?

Strangers: Do you need to look at things from a different perspective or find out more about yourself?

Sun: Do you believe in yourself? You should do as the sun is the symbol of power, energy and success.

Teeth: Do you need a dental check-up? Are you happy

with the image you present to the world? Do you need to develop your bite and be a bit more assertive?

Telephones: Do you need to listen to what is being said to you? Or are you too talkative? Are you finding it hard to express yourself? Do you need to find a friend or relative to confide in?

Theatre: This is all about recognition. Are you longing to be noticed in real life?

Tigers: Tigers are associated with power and strength so perhaps your dream is reinforcing your own abilities?

Toilet: Do you need to use one? Are you feeling vulnerable right now? Is it time to have a tidy up and get rid of some clutter?

Trains: Trains represent your journey through life and the present phase you are in. Are you sitting, standing, on time, being jostled? All the details will give you clues to the meaning.

Trapped/tunnels: Do you feel constrained in waking life? Do you feel stuck in a relationship? Do others have too much power over your life? Do you long to break free?

Trees: Trees represent your life force. Is the tree healthy and strong or wilting?

Umbrella: Water represents feelings so the umbrella could indicate that whatever happens in real life you will rise above it. If your umbrella is damaged perhaps you are feeling sensitive?

Underwear: Are you afraid of feeling uncomfortable, exposed or vulnerable?

Unemployment/failing exams: Do you feel inadequate and that your talents are not being recognized? Are you making the most of your skills?

Uniform: Uniforms tend to be associated with rules and authority. Are you happy wearing your uniform in your dream?

University: Have you got all the facts? Do you need to seek out more information or get some advice about something or someone?

Vampire: Do you feel drained and depleted by demands at school and home? Do love and relationships scare you?

Vegetables: How's your diet these days?

Volcano: Is the volcano active or dormant? Are you about to erupt or have past troubles died down?

Vomit: Have you upset someone? Do you lack self-worth? Have you just had a clear out or are you finally getting over a break up with your boyfriend?

Waitress: Do you think of your own needs as much as you do others? Are you the waitress or are other people taking care of you?

Walking: Are you moving steadily towards your goals?

Walls: Are there obstacles and challenges facing you? Is someone blocking your way right now?

Water: Water often symbolizes your feelings. Is the water clear, murky, deep? Is there too much or too little of it? Are you drowning or swimming?

Swimming often suggests how well you are coping with your emotions. Do you need to reconsider how you are handling a situation? If you dream of boiling water is it time you let off steam?

Window: What's your current view on life? What do you see?

Wolves: Do you need to watch out for someone you know? Is someone bringing you new ideas and information?

X-ray: Do you need to examine something at a deeper level? Is there someone or something you need to see through? Are you afraid of others seeing the real you?

Xylophone: Musical instruments often indicate a change in your lifestyle. What kind of instrument are you playing? Are you in tune?

Youths/children: Are you fighting against the reality of growing up? Are you living in the past?

Zebras: Animals frequently reflect your inner drives. If you see a zebra ask yourself if it is aggressive or gentle. Its behaviour could represent a part of your character that you need to take a closer look at.

Zinc: Are you making great progress right now? Are you enjoying the feeling of success?

Zoo: Dreaming of a zoo can help you understand your inner desires and instincts. What condition is the zoo in? Are the animals maltreated or healthy?

 These are just a snapshot of the most commonly occurring symbols in dreams – it's impossible to list them all. Don't take the symbols too literally or solely rely on a dream dictionary. Just use the dictionary as a reference point to get you thinking along the right lines. Your dreams raise many questions, and no dictionary will be able to address them all – it's you who must search within yourself to find the answers.

Dare to dream

No-one has ever achieved anything from the smallest to the greatest unless the dream was dreamed first. Laura Ingalls Wilder (writer, 1867-1957)

Okay, now you have started to interpret your dream messages what do you do about them? If your dreams have highlighted problems or issues you may decide it's time to discuss them with your friends, your family, or your teachers. You may decide to change your lifestyle in some way or your approach to school and family life. Your dreams have hinted to you what needs to change or how you can move forward. Now it's up to you to think about how to remove any obstacles and take action.

Maybe some of your deepest hopes and desires seem unlikely to come true any time soon.

That's fine. Dreams should be a little out of reach. They are supposed to push you to your limits. But if you stay focused and actively work towards them you stand an excellent chance of making them real.

In all this never forget that you are the dreamer. The dream messages come from your mind. You are the one with the power to make positive changes in your life. You must make your own choices and decisions. It is your life. You are the writer, producer and director and you are playing all the roles. Create what you really want!

Your dream messages help you look at the thought patterns that are governing your life. Their whole purpose is to help you understand yourself and find out exactly what makes you tick. Always remember, though, that as fascinating as dreams are, they are not nearly as amazing as you! So concentrate on your real life, use what you learn from your dreams wisely in conjunction with your common sense, intuition and good judgement and live your life to the full. Find the courage to trust yourself and act on your inner convictions. Be bold. Be beautiful. Dare to dream.

Index